Purgatory

Purgatory Tales

True Stories of Souls Manifesting from the Beyond

by

Andrzej Sarwa

Amazon Edition

Introduction

Purgatorial tales are accounts and narratives that revolve around the experiences and encounters related to Purgatory. These stories often describe the struggles, sufferings, and redemptive journeys of souls in the state of purification after death. They provide insights into the nature of Purgatory, its purpose, and the means through which souls can attain their ultimate salvation.

These tales often depict encounters between the living and the souls in Purgatory, highlighting the importance of prayers, offerings, and acts of mercy on behalf of the departed. They serve as reminders of the need for compassion, repentance, and spiritual growth in order to assist these souls on their path towards eternal union with God.

Purgatorial tales can be both enlightening and thought-provoking, urging individuals to reflect on the transient nature of life, the reality of divine justice, and the significance of intercessory prayers. They provide glimpses into the spiritual realm and offer hope for the redemption and liberation of souls through the power of God's mercy.

Throughout history, numerous accounts of purgatorial experiences and visitations have been recorded, offering readers a deeper understanding of the afterlife and the ongoing purification process that souls undergo. These tales serve as a source of inspiration for believers, encouraging them to lead virtuous lives, seek reconciliation, and offer prayers and sacrifices for the souls in Purgatory.

In reading and reflecting upon purgatorial tales, individuals are reminded of the interconnectedness of the mystical body of Christ, where the living and the deceased are bound together in prayer and charity. They emphasize the importance of solidarity and communal support in aiding the souls on their journey towards heavenly glory.

Purgatorial tales, with their rich imagery and poignant narratives, serve as reminders of the mercy, love, and justice of God. They invite individuals to ponder the eternal realities and the ultimate destiny of every soul, inspiring them to live with faith, hope, and charity, always mindful of the need to assist and pray for those who are still undergoing purification in Purgatory.

Purgatory, according to Catholic belief, is a temporary state of purification for souls who have died in a state of grace but still have some remaining attachment to sin. During their time in Purgatory, these souls undergo purification to prepare them for the fullness of heavenly glory. Throughout history, there have been numerous accounts and stories related to Purgatory and the experiences of souls in this realm. These purgatorial tales often depict encounters with souls seeking prayers, assistance, or redemption from the living.

These stories describe visions, apparitions, and revelations where individuals claim to have interacted with souls in Purgatory. The souls often appear to the living, requesting prayers, sacrifices, or acts of mercy to alleviate their suffering and expedite their release from Purgatory.

Such tales serve as a reminder of the importance of prayer, intercession, and acts of charity for the souls in Purgatory. They emphasize the belief in the communion of saints and the spiritual bond between the living and the dead.

While purgatorial tales may vary in their details and specific accounts, they share a common theme of souls in need of assistance and the power of prayer and good works to aid them in their journey towards heavenly perfection.

These stories, although often considered within the realm of spirituality and personal faith, have captivated the imagination and devotion of many believers throughout history, providing a glimpse into the mystery and reality of the afterlife and the transformative power of God's mercy.

Death Is Not The End Of Existence

According to the teachings of the Catholic Church, earthly human life is just a stage on the way to eternity. Therefore, one should not show more interest in material goods than is necessary.

A human being is composed of two interdependent elements: the material body and the immaterial soul. The former, whose existence is strictly conditioned by its connection to the latter, is subject to death and subsequent destruction. The soul, however, continues to live after leaving the body, as it is inherently immortal. Although it retains all the psychic attributes of a living human being, it is not fully the same because it no longer has any possibility of acting on the material plane.

Death, therefore (or in other words, the cessation of all bodily life functions), is not the final end of existence but a change in the form of existence. Time-bound existence comes to an end and eternity begins.

A human being stands on the border of two worlds: the material, as the perishable body resembles animals, and the spiritual, as the immortality of the soul resembles angels and even

God Himself. Once, at the beginning of time, the Creator endowed the first humans with immortality, conditioning it, however, on their absolute submission to the established law. At the same time, Adam and Eve possessed free will, the ability to choose their actions, and they could either keep this law and live forever or transgress it and die.

That's when Satan entered the stage of humanity. Once the most beautiful of angels, but due to his rebellion against God - driven by pride - he became the ugliest and filled with hatred towards the Creator.

Since losing his position in Paradise, he has been seizing every opportunity to spite God and he decided to use the First Parents for this purpose. Since God said:

"..But of the tree of the knowledge of good and evil, thou shalt not eat of it: for in the day that thou eatest thereof thou shalt surely die.." (Genesis 2:17 - KJV)

He immediately contradicted and said:

"And the serpent said unto the woman, Ye shall not surely die: For God doth know that in the day ye eat thereof, then your eyes shall be opened, and ye shall be as gods, knowing good and evil." (Genesis 3:4-5 - KJV)

Adam and Eve believed the serpent, and as a result, they lost their immortality because:

"For the wages of sin is death." (Romans 6:23 - KJV)

And by the law of succession, the necessity of death passed on to all their descendants, and as the Church teaches, there is no one who is exempt from this law. Even Lord Jesus, when He assumed human flesh, subjected Himself to it.

And by the law of succession, the necessity of dying passed to all their descendants, and - as the Church teaches - there is no one who is not subject to this law. Even the Lord Jesus, the moment He took on human flesh, surrendered to it.

Therefore, everyone must die. This also entails a significant element of uncertainty: When? Today, tomorrow, in twenty years? Since the moment of death cannot be predicted, one should live in such a way as to be constantly prepared for it. So, how should one do this in order to fulfill this condition? The most complete answer can be found in the Gospel of Saint Luke, where Jesus tells a parable about a certain rich man who had a bountiful harvest. He pondered within himself, saying:

"And he spake a parable unto them, saying, The ground of a certain rich man brought forth plentifully: And he thought within himself, saying, What shall I do, because I have no room where to bestow my fruits? And he said, This will I do: I will pull down my barns, and build greater; and there will I bestow all my fruits and my goods. And I will say to my soul, Soul, thou hast much goods laid up for many years; take thine ease, eat, drink, and be merry. But God said unto him, Thou fool, this night thy soul shall be required of thee: then whose shall those things be, which thou hast provided? So is he that layeth up treasure for himself, and is not rich toward God". (Luke 12:16-21-KJV)

A Christian should live differently: prioritizing spiritual values above material ones. The fact that throughout history (and even currently) not everyone has followed the evangelical commandments is another matter. Nevertheless, this understanding of temporality as a stage on the path to eternity is a cornerstone of Catholic doctrine and reflects its eschatological nature.

Although the law of death is universal, and it must come within a certain span of years, the Bible informs us that it has been suspended for an immensely long time for two individuals. These individuals are Enoch and Elijah. Regarding Enoch, we read in the Book of Genesis:

And all the days of Enoch were three hundred sixty and five years: And Enoch walked with God: and he was not; for God took him. (Genesis 5:23-24 - KJV)

As for the other individual, he was taken up to heaven in a fiery chariot while still in his physical body. A vivid description of this event can be found in the Scriptures:

"And it came to pass, when the LORD would take up Elijah into heaven by a whirlwind, that Elijah went with Elisha from Gilgal. And Elijah said unto Elisha, Tarry here, I pray thee; for the LORD hath sent me to Bethel. And Elisha said unto him, As the LORD liveth, and as thy soul liveth, I will not leave thee. So they went down to Bethel. And the sons of the prophets that were at Bethel came forth to Elisha, and said unto him, Knowest thou that the LORD will take away thy master from thy head to day? And he said, Yea, I know it; hold ye your peace. And Elijah said unto him, Elisha, tarry here, I pray thee; for the LORD hath sent me to Jericho. And he said, As the LORD liveth, and as thy soul liveth, I will not leave thee. So they came to Jericho. And the sons of the

prophets that were at Jericho came to Elisha, and said unto him, Knowest thou that the LORD will take away thy master from thy head to day? And he answered, Yea, I know it; hold ye your peace. And Elijah said unto him, Tarry, I pray thee, here; for the LORD hath sent me to Jordan. And he said, As the LORD liveth, and as thy soul liveth, I will not leave thee. And they two went on. And fifty men of the sons of the prophets went, and stood to view afar off: and they two stood by Jordan. And Elijah took his mantle, and wrapped it together, and smote the waters, and they were divided hither and thither, so that they two went over on dry ground. And it came to pass, when they were gone over, that Elijah said unto Elisha, Ask what I shall do for thee, before I be taken away from thee. And Elisha said, I pray thee, let a double portion of thy spirit be upon me. And he said, Thou hast asked a hard thing: nevertheless, if thou see me when I am taken from thee, it shall be so unto thee; but if not, it shall not be so. And it came to pass, as they still went on, and talked, that, behold, there appeared a chariot of fire, and horses of fire, and parted them both asunder; and Elijah went up by a whirlwind into heaven. And Elisha saw it, and he cried, My father, my father, the chariot of Israel, and the horsemen thereof. And he saw him no more: and he took hold of his own clothes, and rent them in two pieces. He took up also the mantle of Elijah that fell from him, and went back, and stood by the bank of Jordan; And he took the mantle of Elijah that fell from him, and smote the waters, and said, Where is the LORD God of Elijah? and when he also had smitten the waters, they parted hither and thither: and Elisha went over". (2 Kings 2:11–KJV)

These two prophets – Enoch and Elijah, God kept alive until the end times. Fr. Marcin Ziółkowski in his *Eschatology* writes:

"According to tradition, these two Old Testament men have not yet died, but are living somewhere in a place known to God. "We do not doubt," says St. Augustine – that Enoch and Elijah live in the bodies in which they were born. Before the end of the world, they are to reappear on earth to prepare everyone for the second coming of Christ by preaching the teaching of Christ and calling people to repentance. Their special mission on earth will fall during the reign of the Antichrist and the general apostasy of people from the principles of faith. Hence, according to the Fathers of the Church, Enoch and Elijah are to fight the fight against the Antichrist and are to die a martyr's death in this fight. "Enoch and Elijah are alive," says St. Augustine – they have been transferred, and wherever they are, they live. And if we are not mistaken by a certain assumption of faith from the Scriptures of God, then they are to die. For the Apocalypse mentions two miraculous prophets that they will die and in the presence of people will rise from the dead and ascend to the Lord. By them is meant Enoch and Elijah, although their names are silenced there". (Ks. M. Ziółkowski, *Eschatologia*, Sandomierz 1963, p. 23).

Thus, we already know the Catholic view of death, its inevitability and, at the same time, the immortality of the soul. What, then, awaits a man after crossing this border separating two worlds: the temporal and the eternal?

Detailed Judgment – It Will Reveal The Deeds Of The Soul, Weigh And Pass Judgment

Immediately after the soul departs from the lifeless body, it stands before the face of Christ for judgment. All of a person's deeds, both good and evil, are revealed, and a moral evaluation of the deceased takes place, followed by the pronouncement of judgment. For a life that was good, filled with love for the Creator and neighbor, there is reward, but for a life that was evil, filled with hatred and self-worship, there is punishment. At the moment of death, the possibility of any further change in one's destiny ends because the merit and guilt have reached their final limit, which stems from two reasons. Firstly, the soul, detached from the body, is no longer the complete human being it was intended to be in God's plan at the moment of creation. Deprived of its material form, with which it formed a psychophysical unity, it can no longer act. Secondly, the time designated for choosing between God and Satan has come to an end.

Should the detailed judgment be understood as analogous to a human, earthly court, where there are judges, the accused, the prosecutor, the defense, and a specific legal procedure? Certainly not. Instead, it is the soul that, upon being shown its entire life, engages in self-evaluation, becoming aware of its choices, and God confirms it with His authority.

This is what Rev. Marcin Ziółkowski writes about the detailed judgment:

"The matter of the detailed judgment encompasses all thoughts, words, and actions, starting from the moment when a person began to use reason and free will, thereby discerning good and evil. Thus, the entirety of a person's moral life is subject to the detailed judgment; whatever good or evil a person has done in this life, their soul must give an account of it in the divine judgment. The strictness and righteousness of this judgment can be inferred from the words of Christ:

"But I say unto you, That every idle word that men shall speak, they shall give account thereof in the day of judgment. For by thy words thou shalt be justified, and by thy words thou shalt be condemned". (Matthew 12:36-37 - KJV).

The detailed judgment takes place through a special divine enlightenment that unveils and presents to the soul its entire moral life. At the moment of separation from the body, the soul receives infused cognitive ideas and special light from God. Through these infused cognitive ideas, strengthened by the action of divine light, the soul intuitively and clearly comprehends its entire moral state, including all its merits and sins. All the good or evil thoughts, words, and actions from earthly life come to light. The illuminating divine light in the soul's mind is so powerful that through it, the soul compre-

15

hends with utmost accuracy and detail everything good or evil it has accomplished in the body on Earth.

Likewise, the pronouncement of judgment occurs through a special divine enlightenment. The soul intuitively and precisely apprehends its moral state, realizing that it is being judged by God at that moment and receives the judgment it deserves. The judgment pronounced in the detailed judgment is immediately executed. The soul (...) immediately enters its designated place (...). The place of the detailed judgment is the place of death. Where a person dies, there also does the divine judgment over their soul take place. (...) At the moment of judgment, the soul does not directly perceive its judge - Christ (...). However, through the special divine enlightenment, the soul has perfect awareness that Christ is judging it at that moment and passing judgment upon it. (Ks. Marcin Ziółkowski, *Eschatologia*, Sandomierz 1963, pp. 130-132)

Now begins the next part of existence, lasting from the moment of judgment until the day of the resurrection of the bodies and the Last Judgment. Although souls have been separated from the material world, they have retained a certain bond with it. This is taught by the dogma of the communion of saints, emphasizing the unity of the earthly and extraterrestrial Churches. The living can help the dead by praying for them, and vice versa. Of course, the damned are excluded from this unity, because neither can they be helped nor are they able and unwilling to help the living. Self-absorbed, despairing and hell-suffering from fire and hatred - hating both God and themselves to the point of pain.

And When You Die, You Will Receive Your Payment

As I mentioned earlier, the judgment that takes place over the human soul after death is not at all like the judgment we know from earthly life.

It is an official - in the face of Christ - confirmation of the choice that man made while living on earth. This is due to the free will that the human race was endowed with at the moment of creation. God, giving man the freedom to choose an action, also gave him reason, which allows him to distinguish which action will lead where: to eternal happiness or to eternal torment.

If he lives in accordance with the law given by the Creator, he chooses heaven, and if he consciously and voluntarily breaks and exceeds this law, he chooses hell. It can be compared to a child who is instructed by a mother: "Don't play with the knife," she says, "or you'll cut yourself." The child may or may not listen to it, and therefore may or may not injure himself.

More than two hundred years ago, Father Karol Fabiani put it this way:

"If you say, I have been in so many occasions and dangers in which it was impossible for me to guard against sin and to avoid it, they will answer you, or you did not know that God admonished and warned: *Qui amat periculum, in illo peribit* (who loves in danger, in danger will die)? You've been on so many occasions, who told you to be there? You yourself have been looking for an opportunity for evil, you have exposed yourself to it. So you too are lost". (Ks. K. Fabiani, *Kazania niedzielne całego roku...*, Kalisz 1786, pp. 48-49).

Because God, out of love for man, does not deprive him of the right to freedom, always respecting it, even when man – from God's point of view – misuses it and, as a result, leads to tragedy, God cannot be accused of cruelty.

The greatest good of man is freedom, and God respects this freedom.

So we already know that where we are after death is entirely up to us. And according to Catholic teaching, you can find yourself in three places: heaven, purgatory or hell.

Let's look at purgatory:

Purgatory

The Catholic Church teaches about Purgatory, which is a state rather than a place in the afterlife where the souls of all those people reside for a certain designated period of time. These are the souls of those who, although they did not die in a state of mortal sin, were either tainted by venial sins or did not have the opportunity to suffer the punishments they were due for their transgressions while still living on Earth. For the justice of God, there is no merit without reward, just as there is no fault without punishment.

Since nothing imperfect can enter the abodes of heavenly bliss, it seems logical that God should have created Purgatory —a place of expiation for minor offenses, a place where the souls of the deceased can completely purify themselves within a certain period of time in order to attain the heavenly reward.

Therefore, Purgatory is necessary for divine justice. But it is also necessary for divine love. It is precisely that love which allows the souls, for whom even the slightest transgression or unpaid debt closed the path to heaven, to rid themselves of the burden dragging them down and, ultimately, after undergoing penance, to be fully united with God.

The Catholic Church teaches that the living can assist the souls in Purgatory through prayers, fasting, good deeds, offering Holy Mass for their intentions, and participating in the Eucharist.

And on what does the Church base its teaching about Purgatory?

Although the word "purgatory" does not appear even once in the Old or New Testament of Sacred Scripture, its existence can be inferred from various biblical texts, which I will now quote:

Wherefore I say unto you, All manner of sin and blasphemy shall be forgiven unto men: but the blasphemy against the Holy Ghost shall not be forgiven unto men. And whosoever speaketh a word against the Son of man, it shall be forgiven him: but whosoever speaketh against the Holy Ghost, it shall not be forgiven him, neither in this world, neither in the world to come. (Matthew 12:31-32 – KJV)

According to the grace of God which is given unto me, as a wise masterbuilder, I have laid the foundation, and another buildeth thereon. But let every man take heed how he buildeth thereupon. For other foundation can no man lay than that is laid, which is Jesus Christ. Now if any man build upon this foundation gold, silver, precious stones, wood, hay, stubble; Every man's work shall be made manifest: for the day shall declare it, because it shall be revealed by fire; and the fire shall try every man's work of what sort it is. If any man's work abide which he hath built thereupon, he shall receive a reward. If any man's work shall be burned, he shall suffer loss: but he himself shall be saved; yet so as by fire. (1 Corinthians 3:10-15 - KJV)

And that servant, which knew his lord's will, and prepared not himself, neither did according to his will, shall be beaten with many stripes. But he that knew not, and did commit things worthy of stripes, shall be beaten with few stripes. For unto whomsoever much is given, of him shall be much required: and to whom men have committed much, of him they will ask the more. (Luke 12:47-48 - KJV)

And his lord was wroth, and delivered him to the tormentors, till he should pay all that was due unto him. So likewise shall my heavenly Father do also unto you, if ye from your hearts forgive not every one his brother their trespasses. (Matthew 18:34-35 KJV)

Agree with thine adversary quickly, whiles thou art in the way with him; lest at any time the adversary deliver thee to the judge, and the judge deliver thee to the officer, and thou be cast into prison. Verily I say unto thee, Thou shalt by no means come out thence, till thou hast paid the uttermost farthing. (Matthew 5:25-26 - KJV)

The Apostle Saint Paul in that passage from the First Letter to the Corinthians seems to be speaking about the fact that the lives of individual Christians can be different, based on one of the possible foundations they accept - Jesus Christ. Their achievements can indeed vary greatly, from great and glorious ones to insignificant ones that will not withstand the test and will be consumed by fire. However, even though the people

whose deeds are consumed by fire will suffer loss, they themselves will be purified through that fire.

Since the assessment of human achievements will only hap-
pen after death, the purification by fire does not occur during
life but after transitioning into immortality.

In addition to the New Testament passages quoted above,
Catholic theologians also refer to the words contained in the
Second Book of Maccabees. Here is the part we are interested
in:

*So Judas gathered his host, and came into the city of Odollam,
And when the seventh day came, they purified themselves, as the
custom was, and kept the sabbath in the same place. And upon the
day following, as the use had been, Judas and his company came to
take up the bodies of them that were slain, and to bury them with
their kinsmen in their fathers' graves. Now under the coats of every one that was slain they found things consecrated to the idols of
the Jamnites, which is forbidden the Jews by the law. Then every
man saw that this was the cause wherefore they were slain. All
men therefore praising the Lord, the righteous Judge, who had
opened the things that were hid, Betook themselves unto prayer,
and besought him that the sin committed might wholly be put out of
remembrance. Besides, that noble Judas exhorted the people to
keep themselves from sin, forsomuch as they saw before their eyes
the things that came to pass for the sins of those that were slain.
And when he had made a gathering throughout the company to
the sum of two thousand drachms of silver, he sent it to Jerusalem
to offer a sin offering, doing therein very well and honestly, in that
he was mindful of the resurrection: For if he had not hoped that
they that were slain should have risen again, it had been superflu-*

ous and vain to pray for the dead. And also in that he perceived that there was great favour laid up for those that died godly, it was an holy and good thought. Whereupon he made a reconciliation for the dead, that they might be delivered from sin. (2 Maccabees 12, 38-45 -KJV)

The passage above is meant to demonstrate that the forgiveness of sins is also possible after death, which is used to justify the Catholic teaching on purgatory. However, theologians, when teaching about purgatory, refer not only to the Bible but also to the early Christian tradition, specifically the custom of praying for the dead. This is what Christians did in the early centuries of the Church:

They express this through fervent, and sometimes restless, desires for refreshment for those souls, defense against evil, and liberation from darkness. They express it even more clearly by praying for them and requesting prayers for them from all sides, understanding that these souls are in a state where something is lacking and they need help. Most clearly, they show their belief in purgatory through the distinction they make among souls: they do not pray at all for children who, after baptism, go to God without the stain of sin, nor for those who, through martyrdom, have been perfectly cleansed like a second baptism. Therefore, when they pray for others, it is because they suspect the possibility of sins not completely eradicated in them. (Ks. J. Morawski, *Świętych obcowanie*, part 1, Communion among Souls, Krakow 1904, p. 99-100)

Because, according to divine revelation, there is no merit or guilt after death, and thus a person on their own is unable to

change their fate and immediately after the particular judgment goes to their final destination, if there were no place
where it is possible to be purified of venial sins or to undergo
incomplete punishments, all prayers for the dead would have
no meaning and would have no effect. Meanwhile, for centuries, the Church has been praying for the deceased in their
sins. It also teaches that the living, through their prayers and
other devout practices performed to alleviate the sufferings of
those in purgatory, can not only bring them relief but also
shorten the time of waiting to see God in eternity.

Can The Deceased Manifest Themselves To The Living?

I t is obvious and understandable that after the death of the body, the connection between the soul of the deceased and the living people is forever severed, at least in the temporal, material dimension. The world of the living and the world of the dead are separated from each other as much as existence in time is separated from existence in eternity. But... Yes, but... Could it be that in certain particular cases, God allows the souls in purgatory to contact the living, with a clearly defined purpose that undoubtedly also serves the spiritual (and even temporal) good of the living?

It is not for us to delve into God's plans, nor to judge God's decisions. Nevertheless, for centuries, devotional literature has been filled with descriptions of encounters between the souls of the departed and the living. This includes souls that go straight to heaven, as well as those condemned to purgatory for purification and even those condemned to eternal damnation and cast into the depths of hell.

Some of these accounts of encounters between the living and the dead may bring a smile to our faces, as they may seem naive. But does their naivety immediately undermine their credibility? How else can one tell in a accessible, vivid, and fear-inspiring way about the torments suffered on the other side of life or even simply testify to the existence of this other reality? Isn't it necessary to adapt such storytelling to the mentality of the listeners, using expressions and comparisons that are understandable and tailored to their intellectual level and knowledge?

In the 19th century, even among theologians, there was a trend towards rationally explaining miraculous phenomena. Miracles and revelations became something shameful, better left unspoken in order to avoid being ridiculed by so-called progressive people or ordinary skeptics.

However, miracles and revelations (permitted by God), including those involving the souls in purgatory, do not take place for the purpose of providing sensations and entertainment. The fact that God allows them has deeper roots aimed at the spiritual good of humanity and serves as a reminder of our duty to help the souls suffering in purgatory.

Tales of souls in penance in cemeteries, old castles, churches, or monasteries have long been dismissed as not only harmful fairy tales for the faithful living, but also for those who are in purgatory. Is it right to do so? It is not for me to judge, and I leave the resolution of this issue to more competent individuals. However, allow me to pose a question for which I do not expect an answer: Is purgatory a state of souls, a place where they reside, or perhaps both? Can we absolutely exclude the possibility that purgatorial punishments can also be undergone on Earth, albeit in a different dimension, distinct from our familiar temporal realm?

But the time has come to present the reader with a handful of stories drawn from ancient devotional literature, which speak of the fact that the world of the living and the world of the dead are much closer to each other than one might think based on observations of the reality surrounding us...

Purgatory Tales

Caring for the soul

Esteemed writer Walenty Wielogłowski recounts: "Peter Gamrat, the bishop of Krakow, had a similar life and penance to St. Mary Magdalene. In his youth, while still a lay-man, he led a dissolute life, having a companion and leader in his misdeeds named Kurosz, also known as Kurozwański. However, touched by the grace of the Holy Spirit, he abandoned his former life and became a priest. He eventually reached the position of the bishop of Krakow. He was merciful to the poor, feeding one hundred of them every day with his own bread, and he always had two wagons loaded with fur coats and other garments following him. So, when he encountered someone destitute or shivering from the cold on the road, he not only clothed them but also gave them gifts. Once, on the eve of a certain feast day, he was preparing to go to church for vespers. While sitting alone in his room, he waited for the signal that the time had come. In the meantime, the figure of a person familiar to him appeared before him, namely, Kurosz, who had died long ago. At first, he became afraid, but after regaining his composure, he asked Kurosz where he came from. He replied:

"I am alive and living a far happier life than you are."

Gamrat responded, "Can it be that you, who led such a debauched life, are saved, which I know very well?"

Kurosz then replied,

"When I was young and in foreign lands, I was in the company of someone who blasphemed and insulted the Blessed Mother. Filled with zeal for her honor, I stood up and bravely defended her. In my subsequent life, I never thought about this matter until the time when my soul was to depart from my body. When I rightly feared the judgment of God, the Most Holy Virgin appeared before me with a retinue of angels and, casting a merciful gaze upon me, said:

Shall my soldier, the defender of my honor, perish? The Most Holy Virgin then interceded for me with her Son, and when this happened, I felt sincere contrition and disgust for my past vices. I no longer pleaded with my lips but with my heart for God's mercy, and He accepted my repentance. When I died in that state, He did not condemn my soul but counted it among His chosen ones. Now He has sent me to you to warn you about the approaching end of your life. Know that in six months, you will surely depart from this world. So, you still have time for penance and reconciling with God.

After saying this, Kurosz disappeared from Gamrat's sight, and Gamrat, shedding tears, began to sincerely contemplate reforming his life and practicing penance. He did not admit anyone to his presence that day and, after a while, confided in his trusted friend about what had happened to him. He devoted himself entirely to penance, and six months later (in 1545), as prophesied, he passed away from this world." (*Co warta dusza. Karta z życia Siostry Dominiki, Szarytki, z czasów wojny Francusko-Pruskiej w 1870 roku*, Warszawa 1930, pp. 23-26).

Memory of Souls about Us

Father Jesuit Mrowiński writes: "In the Gniezno county, there is a village called Czeszewo, which belonged to the late councilor Szuman several decades ago. In his old age, he lost his spouse and lived alone in a quite spacious old Polish manor house because he was childless.

This manor house, like almost all the older ones, was made of wood and had the common peculiarity for those times that it leaked whenever it rained, despite being thatched.

In several places in the rooms, plates were placed on beds, cabinets, and other furniture to catch the dripping water. Naturally, the ceilings and beams suffered greatly from this. - A few weeks after his wife's death, the councilor was sleeping peacefully when suddenly he woke up and saw in the doorway leading to the adjacent room the apparition of his deceased wife. She looked at him kindly and beckoned with her finger for him to get up and approach her. Startled, he lit a candle but, seeing nothing, he didn't bother and muttered to himself, 'Imagination!' He extinguished the candle and fell back asleep.

After a while, the same figure of his wife appeared to him again in the same spot and gestured to him in the same way as before. The councilor lit a candle, but as the vision disappeared, and he was a very level-headed person who didn't believe in any fears, he extinguished the light and fell asleep. After a while, his deceased wife appeared to him for the third time in the same place and gestured to him with great urgency.

The councilor had had enough of this. He lit a candle, put on his dressing gown, and went to the adjacent room where his wife had entered. He searched, shining the light, but found no one. When he somewhat bewilderedly returned to his bedroom, he heard a crash and the sound of beams breaking, followed by the collapse of the ceiling, which crushed the bed and everything else in the bedroom. Overwhelmed by fear, he fell to the ground, and a cloud of dust filled the room where he was. Soon, however, he regained his composure and then recounted this strange event to everyone. I also heard about it from his nephews, highly respected citizens in the Duchy of Poznań, one of whom was the president of the Polish parliamentary circle in Berlin." (*Co warta dusza...*, pp. 27-29).

Miracles of God's mercy through the intercession of the souls in purgatory

Wilhelm Freyszen, a famous bookseller in Cologne, having received two remarkable graces from God in 1649 through the intercession of the souls in purgatory, wrote a letter to Father Jakub Monfort, a zealous promoter of devotion for the deceased, by publishing a book entitled *De misericordia defunctis exhibenda* (*On Showing Mercy to the Departed Souls*). We present this letter in its entirety.

"I am writing to you, Father, to inform you about two miracles that I experienced through God's mercy, namely the healing of my wife and my son. On holidays, my shop is usually closed; therefore, having more time, I started reading a book on devotion for the souls in purgatory, which you kindly entrusted to me for printing. While I was still engrossed in reading, I was informed that my four-year-old boy was seriously ill. After a few days, his condition worsened to the point that doctors had no hope of curing him, and preparations were being made for his funeral. In my deep sorrow, I turned to God, and the thought came to me that I might save him by making a vow for the benefit of the souls in purgatory. The next morning, I went to the church and fervently begged the Lord to listen to me, vowing to distribute a hundred copies of this booklet, which encourages mercy for the suffering Church, free of charge, and to give them to priests and monks so that the practices indicated there would be fulfilled with greater benefit.

I was full of hope. When I returned home, I found my son feeling better; he asked for food, although he couldn't swallow a drop of water for several days. The next day, he was completely healthy, got up, went for a walk, and ate as if he had never been sick. Overwhelmed with gratitude, I tried to fulfill my promise as quickly as possible. I went to the priests, asking them to take as many copies as they wished for themselves and to distribute the rest to priests, monks, and monasteries, so that the souls in purgatory, my benefactors, would find salvation through their prayers..."

(The same man, through the intercession of the souls in purgatory, obtained the healing of his terminally ill wife, but I omit this description as it is very similar to the previous one). (A. Morawski, *Cuda i Łaski Miłosierdzia Bożego*, Warszawa 1892, pp. 12-14)

Almsgiving for the deceased will not go unrewarded

N ot everyone can give great alms, but with goodwill and a small offering, we can support the suffering souls to secure God's blessing. The Gospel widow offered two small coins, which is one penny, into the temple treasury, and Jesus praised her for giving what she could.

This example was followed by a poor Neapolitan woman who could barely feed her small children. Her husband, a poor and devout worker, brought home meager wages from his hard work every evening. Unfortunately, one day this poor father was arrested and imprisoned for debts, and the entire burden of supporting the family fell on the unfortunate mother, who had no other means of living except her own work and trust in God's mercy. Day and night, she fervently prayed to God for deliverance from this misfortune, especially for the release of her husband, who was languishing in prison not for any wrongdoing. The poor woman had no hope of paying off those debts.

She was told about a wealthy citizen who used his wealth to support the unfortunate. Immediately, the poor woman tried to write a request expressing her poverty and asking for the mercy of the kind gentleman. But unfortunately, she received only a small alms—a tiny sum. What should she do and who should she turn to? Saddened and deeply distressed, she went to the church and threw herself at the feet of the Savior hidden in the Most Holy Sacrament, begging for a miracle of mercy for her unfortunate family because hope in people was in vain. Suddenly, as if struck by lightning, a thought came to her, perhaps from her Guardian Angel, to seek the intercession of the souls in purgatory. She had heard from someone about their sufferings and their great gratitude to those who supported them. Comforted by this inspiration, she immediately went to the sacristy, offered her little money, and asked for a Holy Mass to be celebrated for the souls in purgatory. A compassionate priest who happened to be there began the holy sacrifice, with her joining her fervent prayers, lying prostrate on the ground.

Filled with great strength and spiritual comfort from this prayer, as if she was certain that God had heard her, she returned home through the bustling streets of the city. A serious old man approached her and asked, "Why do you look so sad?" She answered with gestures about her distress. The stranger listened to her with sympathy, encouraged her to trust in God, and as he walked away, handed her a letter, asking her to deliver it to the designated person. The poor woman went straight to the indicated place, and finding a young man, the master of the house, she fulfilled the task. Opening the paper, the young man, deeply moved and surprised, recognized the handwriting of his deceased father, who had passed away many years ago...

"Son, your father has been delivered from purgatory today through this poor woman who will give you this letter. A Holy Mass was offered for the souls in purgatory from her offering this morning, and in His mercy, the Lord accepted it for the completion of my purification. Therefore, we owe her the greatest gratitude. This honorable woman is in dire need, and I commend her to your care." (A. Morawski, *Cuda i łaski...*, pp. 16-20).

Needless to say, the son of the father delivered from purgatory generously provided for that poor woman, ensuring that she would never experience scarcity again.

This is another example that the mercy shown to the souls in purgatory brings upon us the miracles of God's mercy.

About soldiers asking for assistance after death

A round the year of Our Lord 1078, near Worms, for many days and nights, great wonders could be observed. A large number of armed men – some on foot, others on horse-back – appeared to the local residents, causing a commotion. It seemed as if these troops were coming out of the nearby mountain.

This event not only aroused astonishment but also fear. However, there was a certain monk, a resident of the Lunxur-gian monastery, who, along with several companions, boldly went out to meet these armed men, wearing a cross around their necks.

Once he asked them who they were, where they came from, and what they desired, he received the following answer:

"We are not a nocturnal apparition, nor are we living peo-ple, but souls who once served mighty lords in this world. Many years ago, in this very place, we perished in a fierce bat-tle."

"And because we led a godless life, we must now suffer pun-ishment."

"Look at us. The clothing, armor, weapons, and horses that served us in life and were often the cause of sin have become the cause of terrible torments after death. Everything you see around us, all of it is fire that burns us, although you cannot see it with your mortal eyes."

When the monk asked if the living could somehow help and provide relief for them, he heard from the same soul of a soldier:

"Through fasting and prayers, and especially through offerings of the Body and Blood of the Lord Jesus, we can be saved, and we ask for that."

When he finished speaking, the whole host of spirits cried out in unison three times:

"Pray for us!"

And immediately it seemed as if they all turned into fire, and even the mountain itself seemed to be burning with fire, thunder resounded in the sky, and the tree crowns rustled loudly.

About the monk who ended up in purgatory
due to negligence in praying for the deceased

In the Convent of the Immaculate Conception in Parma, in the year 1541, a highly devout father named John de Via died, regarded by everyone as extraordinarily holy. During his lifetime, he befriended another devout monk, Brother Ascentius.

After the death of John, Ascentius spent several days in prayer for the peace of his friend's soul, and suddenly a brightness beyond description enveloped him, and from that brightness emerged the figure of the deceased. The terrifying fear seized Ascentius, and he couldn't utter a single word. As this phenomenon continued, eventually he became somewhat accustomed to it and gathered the courage to ask what the deceased demanded of him.

The deceased spoke these words:

"Despite my holy life, fervent prayers, fasting, and penance, I neglected to recite the Office for the deceased. Although God, in His mercy, did not condemn me, I will not achieve eternal glory and pass through the gates of heaven until you, the living in this monastery, fulfill what I failed to fulfill."

After uttering these words, the vision disappeared. Terrified and deeply moved, Brother Ascentius informed the guardian of what had occurred, and without delay, the guardian ordered what the penitent soul of Father John de Via had requested.

After some time, Father John appeared again to his friend, but this time with much greater clarity, thanking him for fulfilling the request, which had such colossal significance for the deceased.

The value of the Holy Sacrifice
for the souls in purgatory

When Father John de Aluerna, a Franciscan, celebrated the Holy Mass on All Souls' Day, offering it with such love and piety that he was almost enraptured, he witnessed an extraordinary vision. As he lifted up the most holy Body of Christ during the Holy Mass, offering it to the Heavenly Father, that He may deign to deliver with His love those who hung on the cross, he saw an countless number of souls emerging from purgatory, as if a multitude of arrows were shooting upwards from a fiery furnace, and he saw them entering the heavenly homeland by the merits of our Lord Jesus Christ, who allowed Himself to be crucified for the salvation of humanity.

On the torments suffered
by unworthy monks in purgatory

There was a certain monk -unfortunately, history has not provided us with his name or the time in which he lived -who, being near death, experienced rapture and was led to a place
where he endured particularly severe torments. What he saw
astonished and terrified him at the same time. He beheld the
figures of demons who, having seized various unworthy
monks, were roasting them over the fires of hell, carefully col-
lecting the sizzling fat that flowed from them and pouring it
over their scorched bodies.

The angel who served as his guide, seeing that he could not
calmly observe these dreadful torments, quickly led him away
to a place of refreshment and said:

"Those whom you saw being roasted in the great fire did
not willingly serve the Lord in fear and trembling. They did
not sufficiently adhere to the discipline of the Rule, and they
prayed without fervor. In the world, they were courtly, mis-
chievous, frequenters of other people's homes, lovers of excess,
lazy, and thoughtless. Therefore, they will not attain eternal
glory until they have paid every last penny to the Lord."

An hour in purgatory feels like an eternity

A certain monk, unfortunately, history did not provide us with his name or the time in which he lived, was nearing death and was overwhelmed with awe as he was led to a place where particularly intense torments are experienced. What he saw filled him with both astonishment and terror. He beheld demonic figures, who, having seized unworthy monks, roasted them evenly over the fire and skillfully collected the dripping fat to pour it over their charred bodies.

An angel, who served as his guide, saw that he could not bear to watch those dreadful torments and promptly led him away to a place of refreshment. The angel then spoke, saying,

"Those whom you saw being scorched in the great fire did not serve the Lord willingly with fear and trembling. They did not sufficiently adhere to the discipline of the Rule, and their prayers lacked fervor. Moreover, in the world, they were worldly, jesters, intruders into others' affairs, lovers of excess, lazy and thoughtless. Therefore, they will not attain eternal glory until they have paid the Lord down to the last penny."

The Hour in Purgatory Seems Like Eternity

A certain monk was on his deathbed, and he requested the abbot, like all others leaving this world, to provide him with the holy sacraments and grant him absolution. However, during that time, the abbot urgently had to leave the monastery, not suspecting that the monk would indeed pass away soon, so he decided to attend to the matter upon his return.

Fate played its role, and in the abbot's absence, the dying monk departed from this world. When the abbot returned, the deceased's body had not yet been buried. With sadness, the abbot thought that he had failed to fulfill the dying monk's request, thus exposing him to suffering after crossing the threshold of life.

However, it happened that the monk had only minor sins and did not deserve eternal damnation, so he could not be cast into the fiery hell. By a special permission from God, the deceased was allowed to appear to the sorrowful abbot, and upon seeing him, the departed one began to demand the promised absolution and the assignment of appropriate penance.

Unaware of what penance to impose on the departed, the abbot said: "As a reparation for your sins, you shall remain in Purgatory until your body is buried."

Upon hearing this, the deceased cried out so cruelly and desperately that his voice resounded throughout the entire abbey. "Oh! You merciless man! You have sentenced me to such prolonged torment. You commanded me to endure for so long in the fire, where time passes altogether differently than in earthly life, and a minute equals centuries."

Having uttered these words, he vanished.

About How Heavy the Torments of Purgatory Are

There was a certain Dominican monk, very devout and pious, who had a close friendship with a certain Franciscan. One day, during a conversation about eternity and life after death in a new reality, they unintentionally made a promise to each other that if it were the will of the Lord, the one who departed from this world first would appear to the one who remained among the living and tell them about their state.

The Franciscan was the first to pass away. After a few days, while the Dominican monk was in the refectory, the deceased appeared to him, and during their brief conversation, he shared some very strange things about the future life, particularly mentioning the immensely heavy torments of Purgatory.

To confirm the truth of these matters, he placed his hand on the table and immediately burned a fiery, deep trace, which can still be seen to this day in the Armorenenian Convent. It serves as evidence that there is life after death and that in this life, those who are deserving must make reparation to Divine Justice.

Purgatory According to St. Frances of Rome

The purgatorial fire is very different from the fires of hell. The latter appeared to St. Frances as a black flame, while the fire in Purgatory is bright and red. She sees – not within Purgatory, but outside – the Guardian Angel on the right and the tempting Devil on the left. The Guardian Angel presents to God the prayers offered by the living for the suffering souls in Purgatory. As for the prayers offered for those souls for whom we presume are in Purgatory but are not there, according to St. Frances, their destiny is as follows: If the soul we think is in Purgatory is already in Heaven and does not need our prayers, the prayer benefits other souls remaining in Purgatory and also benefits the one offering the prayers. However, if the soul we think is in Purgatory is in Hell, the prayer offered for that soul benefits solely the person praying and does not extend to other souls as in the previous case.

St. Frances sees in Purgatory a threefold division of places, each with varying degrees of terror and pain. These parts are further divided into sections. Everywhere, the punishment is proportionate to the sin, its nature, causes, consequences, and other circumstances. (Ernest Hello, *Oblicza świętych*, Warszawa 1910, p. 57).

Purgatory according to St. Joanna of Jesus-Mary

I was also led through Purgatory. "There are equally dreadful torments and sufferings as elsewhere (i.e., in Hell -ed.),
but with the difference that this place is a place of peace, not
damnation. Here, the Lord God is not cursed; instead, He is
praised and blessed. The heaviest suffering for the souls found
there is that they have not yet seen the Lord God. All other
torments are almost the same as in Hell. Oh, if only it could re-
mind and frighten certain people, especially those who lightly
consider certain sins. When they are told about it, they respond that God is not as scrupulous as we are. Oh, how unaware they are of what happens in that world! Everything is
examined there so closely that it would be strange indeed to
witness what happens there, when even one seemingly innocent word spoken in jest is subject to punishment." (*O żywocie
wielebney panny siostry Joanny a Jesu Marya, druk XVII-
wieczny*, p. 67).

How Blessed Sister Joanna of Jesus Mary Helped the Souls in Purgatory.

"Blessed Joanna was extremely merciful and had great love for her neighbors. With her own eyes, she saw and personally experienced the cruel torments of Purgatory [during her earthly life – ed. note].

She also believed that the souls undergoing those torments were friends of God who remained in His grace. Therefore, she had deep compassion for their imprisonment and spared no effort to liberate them from that prison and guide them towards eternal glory. Her afflictions, mortifications, sufferings, and penances were all directed towards the sole purpose of rescuing souls from the torments of Purgatory. The souls in Purgatory would surround Joanna everywhere she went, appearing as rays of sunlight and following her every turn. She recognized each soul as a bride of Christ, marked for Purgatory for many years, and was aware of the sufferings they endured. Sometimes they would surround her and burn her with fire, causing her entire body to burn with intense pain, and her bones to feel as if they were on fire. It was for this reason and due to her personal experience of severe torments in Purgatory that she prayed more fervently and intensely for the souls in Purgatory.

Once, when Christ the Lord revealed to His beloved bride the danger faced by the Spanish kingdom due to its grave and varied sins, she was deeply troubled and sought to appease the Divine Majesty, forgetting about the souls in Purgatory. Then came Good Friday when all the sisters in the monastery celebrated the Passion of Christ, commemorating the solemn devotion. The prioress first entrusted the souls in Purgatory to the sisters. Not hearing it clearly, Joanna asked one of the sisters what the prioress had said. Upon learning that the souls in Purgatory were entrusted to their prayers, she said, 'There are other needs that are more urgent for us; the blessed souls are in a safe place, so let them wait a little.' As soon as Joanna said this, she immediately felt an iron hand of fiery fire wrapping around her arm, almost burning it, causing her to cry out in great pain, 'Fire! I am burning!' This torment lasted for a considerable time. Through this experience, by the righteous permission of God, she herself learned that there is no greater need in the whole world than the need of the souls in Purgatory.

Furthermore, God always revealed to her the severity and exactness of the torments of Purgatory, and He urged her to suffer and pray for those souls. [Pope Urban VIII] appeared to Sister Joanna on the same day he departed from this world. She diligently fulfilled her duties and obligations, to which she had committed herself, and with her prayers, she fervently sought to deliver his soul from Purgatory. The Pope appeared to her, but he was enveloped in immense torments from all sides, making it impossible for her to discern the state of his soul. She never ceased to pray fervently and tearfully for him,

beating herself with various disciplines and lashes, and subjecting herself to many other mortifications. However, she always saw him remaining in that wretched state, and there
seemed to be no consolation for her. At times, when she asked
about his state in subsequent apparitions, he replied that he
did not have permission from God to reveal his state to her.
This answer filled Joanna's heart with heaviness [...]. Therefore, she intensified her prayers and made them more difficult
for the Divine Majesty, but it seemed as if God did not hear
her pleas. Yet, she persisted in her prayers. Christ the Lord,
unable to ignore the pleas of His bride, finally informed her
that the pope's torment could not be shortened and had to be
fulfilled." (From the book *O żywocie wielebney panny...*, pp. 74-
79)

Sister Joanna of Jesus Mary was a Spaniard who lived from
1564 to 1650. She had many mystical experiences.

Purgatory in the Revelations of St. Bridget of Sweden

Saint Bridget of Sweden was the daughter of Birger, a prince from the royal Swedish dynasty, and Sigrid, who also came from the royal house of the Goths. Bridget was born around the year 1303 in Sweden and died in Rome in 1373.

Although she lived in marriage, her life was marked by extraordinary austerity. She prayed extensively and mortified her body in various ways. One particular grace bestowed upon her by the Lord Jesus was the revelations, which were compiled into a large and thick book. These revelations have been recognized by the Church. After her husband's death, Bridget founded a religious order named after her, called the Bridgettines. Her revelations, though challenging and esoteric (some of which may have become outdated), are worth reading as they bring much spiritual benefit.

Examples related to Purgatory, the place and state of suffering souls, are taken precisely from the book of revelations of this great Swedish saint. Some of them may not make a significant impression, while others are even drastic, or rather, horrifying.

"The third place of posthumous existence, as spoken by the Virgin Mary, witnessed by St. Bridget, is Purgatory, and those who are there need threefold mercy because they suffer in three ways. They suffer in hearing because they hear nothing but torment, punishment, and misery; they suffer in seeing because they see nothing but their own wretchedness; they suffer in touch because they feel the unbearable heat of the fire and the weight of punishment. Give them, my Son and Lord, your mercy for the sake of my intercession." The Son answered, "Gladly, for your sake, I will grant them threefold mercy: first, I will alleviate their hearing; their sight will be pacified, and their punishment will diminish and become milder. In the end, whoever, from this hour, is in the greatest torments of Purgatory, will be transferred to moderate or mild ones. And those who are in moderate punishment will receive the mildest punishment, while those who are in the mildest punishment will be transferred to eternal rest." The Mother of God replied, "May honor and eternal glory be to You, my Lord..." (*Skarby Niebieskich Taiemnic to iest Księgi Obiawienia niebieskiego Świętej Matki Brygidy z Rodzaju królewskiego. Xiężnej neryckiey ze Szwecyey. Fundatorki S. Salvatora. Z łacińskiego na polskie przełożone przez Zakonnika Braci Mniejszych Ojców Bernardynów*, Lwów 1698, p. 75).

Vision of Purgatory in the Revelations of St. Bridget

A bove those darknesses - referring to the place of eternal torments, hell - lies the greatest purgatorial punishment that souls can endure. Beyond that place, there are others where the punishment is lesser. It is not merely a deficiency in strength, beauty, and similar things. By way of analogy, I say: just as when someone is sick, and once the illness subsides, they lack the strength to fully recover. The third place, however, is higher, where there is no torment but only a longing to come to God.

On the first place, above the darkness, exists great purgatorial punishment, where she witnessed a soul purifying itself. Demons can be felt there, venomous worms appear in analogy, and the likeness of fierce animals. Heat and cold, darkness and confusion prevail, stemming from the punishment in the lower hell. Some souls experience lesser torments, while others endure greater ones, depending on how much they have amended their sins during the time their soul dwelled with the body" (Treasures of the Heavenly Secrets..., p. 227-228).

On the Terrible Torments of a Soul,
as Seen by St. Bridget

A certain soul had committed much evil in earthly life, and standing before the face of the Most High, by His decree, she had to endure such torments in order to be admitted to eternal light:

"...I saw that as if a certain bundle was tied to her head like a crown, which squeezed so tightly that the back of her head merged with her face; her eyes, however, had fallen out of their sockets and hung by veins until they reached her cheeks; her hair seemed as if burnt by fire and dried up, her brain was being torn and flowing through her nostrils and ears, her tongue was hanging out, and her teeth had fallen out; the bones in her arms were crushed and twisted like cords; her hands were tied around her neck, and her chest and abdomen were so tightly connected to her back that her ribs broke, and her heart, along with all her internal organs, ruptured and burst open; her loins hung on the sides, and her crushed bones protruded and stretched like thin threads. (...)

And the Judge said at that time: for the sake of My Passion, heaven will be opened to her, but she must suffer until she is cleansed from her sins, unless she receives assistance from the good deeds of the living people in the world" (Treasures of the Heavenly Secrets..., p. 227).

Saint Sister Faustina Kowalska sees a soul suffering in torment

S uddenly, "I saw a certain soul that had separated from the body and was in terrible torment. Oh Jesus, when I am to write this, I tremble at the sight of the horrors that testify against it. I saw how from some muddy abyss, the souls of little children and older ones, around the age of nine, were coming out. These souls were repulsive and disgusting, resembling the most terrifying monsters, decaying corpses, yet these corpses were alive and loudly testifying against the soul that I see in agony. And the soul that I see in agony is a soul that was filled with honors and worldly applause, the end of which is emptiness and sin. In the end, a woman came out who held tears as if in her apron, and she testified strongly against it.

Oh dreadful hour, in which one must see all one's actions in complete nudity and wretchedness; not a single one of them perishes, faithfully accompanying us to the judgment of God. I have no words or comparisons to express such terrifying things, and although it seems to me that this soul is not condemned, its torments differ in no way from the torments of hell, except for this difference, that they will someday end" (St. Sister Faustina Kowalska: Diary..., pp. 152-153).

Saint Sister Maria Faustina (in the world, Helena Kowalska), of the Congregation of the Sisters of Our Lady of Mercy, was born on August 25, 1905, in the village of Głogowiec. Since the age of twelve, she felt a calling to consecrated life, but numerous obstacles prevented her from dedicating herself exclusively to the service of God in the Congregation of the Sisters of Our Lady of Mercy until 1926. Throughout her life, she was quiet, humble, and engaged in hard physical work while being spiritually rich. She experienced numerous heavenly revelations, visions of Jesus, and at His command, she promoted the devotion to the Divine Mercy, which has been approved by the Church and spread throughout the world. She passed away in 1938.

The true story of a strange apparition of the deceased.

The story is indeed true, not seen in a dream but in reality, witnessed and attested by reliable witnesses. Here is the miraculous event that took place in the city of Sylwaduk, in the house of Mrs. Dielde, on November 23rd, in the year of Our Lord 1382.

On that very day, the deceased brother of the aforementioned lady appeared in the same attire in which he was laid to rest. He was wearing a black cloak and a velvet undergarment, without a hat. When he lifted the hem of his cloak, a terrifying flame burst forth, causing the witnesses of this marvel to flee.

The deceased's daughters and his sister (the girls' aunt), who were present at the time, understood that it was their own father and brother who had come from the afterlife to appear before them with God's permission. Overcoming their fear, they earnestly asked him what he wished from them and if he could be saved by human assistance. They inquired whether the place where he resides is purgatory or the fiery hell.

While they deliberated on what fate might have befallen him after death, he spoke with a certain reproach in his voice, saying, "And why do you not save me? Why do you fear me? No harm can befall you from my side!"

The girls and their aunt replied, "Out of excessive fear, we hesitate to ask you in detail what you expect from us."

Upon hearing these words, the apparition vanished, and sadness was evident. However, it was not its last appearance to the living. On the same day, around two in the afternoon, the deceased appeared for the second time. For a long time, he uttered not a single word, only sighing heavily and painfully. Finally, he addressed his sister, saying, "Why don't you save me?"

To which she replied, "I am ready to save you by any means recommended by the Church in such cases. Please tell me which ones would be most beneficial and effective for you."

The deceased said, "First, order and ensure that three masses are offered for me. Then go to the city of Orchot and, at the altar of the Holy Cross in the church, make a monetary offering that I had promised when I was sick for the intention of my recovery but neglected to fulfill after regaining my strength. This neglect is a great torment and burden for me in purgatory. Lastly, he asked his daughters and brother to pray for him."

The deceased also mentioned that as long as his sister did not fulfill everything he had asked of her, he would not leave her for a moment, accompanying her day and night. And so it happened. He went with her to the church, where he ensured that she made the monetary offering he had mentioned earlier. She devoutly attended three masses, and they returned to their place of residence together.

He attempted to converse with her, but she no longer wanted to listen to his words or respond to them. All of this lasted from Monday morning until Saturday dawn.

On Saturday, when the sky was barely turning rosy, the deceased awakened his sister and commanded her to dress and go to the church of St. John to adore the Most Holy Sacrament on his behalf. He also said, "Hurry, for my time is short."

And when she, being a woman, was taking too long to dress, he urged her, "Hurry! Hurry! For I will not be here much longer."

Upon stepping into the courtyard, he gave his sister a final instruction to implore their brother and nieces on his behalf, that they should always remain steadfast in the Catholic faith and never neglect to pray for the deceased, for such prayers are of great help and bring great relief from suffering. He also added that his purgatorial torments had lasted for five years but, thanks to the prayers of faithful friends and family and by God's mercy, they had been significantly shortened. He concluded his speech with the words, "Now I am saved for eternity!" After uttering these words, he disappeared.

How St. Christina Penance to Relieve the Suffering of Souls in Purgatory

The story of St. Christina goes as follows: After her death, the angels led her to heaven, where the Lord allowed her to see a dreadful dungeon full of human souls suffering terrifying torments, in accordance with divine justice. She was informed that it was Purgatory.

Later, she was brought before the face of Jesus Christ, who asked her if, having entered eternity in a state of sanctifying grace, she would like to stay in heaven forever or, out of compassion for the poor souls enduring such great suffering, she would voluntarily choose to return to life and undertake severe penances to alleviate the pains and duration of the souls in Purgatory.

Moved by pity for those wretched souls, St. Christina, with great mercy, told the Lord that she chose to return to earth. Her wish was granted.

As soon as she awakened from her mortal sleep, she began to throw herself into burning furnaces, lay in fires, and immerse herself in boiling water. During winter, she would stay under the ice for hours, exposing only her head to be able to breathe.

But that's not all! She would lie among decaying and putre-fying bodies in graves, subjecting herself to even more severe mortifications.

And here is something extraordinary: Despite subjecting herself to such torture and enduring immense pain that often made her cry out, her body remained unharmed, without the slightest trace of wounds, burns, or frostbite. Numerous wit-nesses can attest to this, and we have no reason to doubt them, especially since God has performed even greater miracles in our time than those accomplished through St. Christina, this great friend and advocate of the souls in Purgatory.

The Heavy Torment of a Monk who, Unworthy of It, Desired to Become a Deacon

There was a certain monk from the Cistercian order, renowned for leading a good and pious life, who departed from this world when the time came. Shortly after his death, while the monk responsible for the sacristy was preparing for his nightly rest in his cell, a vision appeared before his eyes. It was the form of the recently deceased monk, who spoke these words:

"Oh, sacristan, I am the brother who recently passed away. I have come to you for a reason. Know that, while still in the flesh, I desired to attain the grace of diaconate out of ambition. This sin is now the cause of my current suffering and penance."

He paused for a moment and then continued:

"But the merciful Lord allowed me to appear to you and ask for your help, which I implore through God's mercy. Go quickly to the father prior and tell him what you have seen and heard. Request the entire assembly to pray for my intention. And to prove that you are not a victim of deception, show him the place where the Psalter is, the same Psalter he has been searching for fruitlessly."

After uttering these words, the vision vanished.

The sacristan, being a sensible man and not inclined to believe in every vision, extinguished the candle, lay down on his cot, and soon fell into a deep slumber. The next day, he said nothing about what he had witnessed to the prior or the other brothers in the monastery.

However, the following night arrived. The sacristan, as before, prepared for sleep, and lo and behold! The apparition of his deceased brother returned, reproaching him and urging him not to disregard the matter any longer, but to disclose everything to the prior.

"As a sign that I am not an illusion, take this Psalter from my hand, the same one that has not been found yet," said the vision.

The sacristan attempted to grab the hand of the specter, but his fingers passed through the air, finding no tangible substance. Now, fully convinced of the reality of the phenomenon, at daybreak, he went to the prior and the other brothers, recounting all that he had seen and heard and presenting the long-lost Psalter as proof.

As one would expect, thanks to numerous masses, offerings, and good deeds, the soul of the suffering brother was delivered from Purgatory and led to eternal glory.

The Souls of the Deceased Joyfully Welcome Those Who Supported Them in Life

In Britain, there was a peasant who, despite being constantly occupied with work, remained devout and never neglected God's commandments and the church. He had a commendable habit: every time he passed by the church or walked through the cemetery, he would pray for the souls resting there. Since everyone's life has a beginning and an end, the final hour also arrived for that peasant.

He requested that the parish priest be brought to him with the Holy Sacrament so that he could be prepared for the journey to eternity. However, since it was nighttime and the priest was lazy, he instructed the deacon, who assisted him in parish work, to administer the Holy Communion to the dying man. The deacon took the Body of Christ and went to the dying man, nourishing him with it. Soon after, the peasant breathed his last.

The deacon had nothing else to do but return to the rectory. However, as he passed by the church, he noticed that its doors were wide open, and a loud voice came from the nearby cemetery, calling out:

"Arise, faithful ones! All of you! And do so quickly! Rise from your graves, all of you who rest in this cemetery! Let us all go to the church and commend the soul of this deceased man, who just passed away, to the mercy of God. For during his lifetime, he never forgot about us, as he always sighed for us to the Lord when passing through the cemetery."

Then a great thunder resounded, and the dead began to emerge from their graves. They entered the brightly illuminated church, lit by hundreds of candles that no one knew who or when had lit them. There, they offered solemn prayers for the soul of the departed peasant, and afterwards, each one returned to their eternal resting place.

The deacon, whether he wanted to or not, witnessed all of this, as such great fear paralyzed him, preventing him from moving. This vision made such an impression on him that he immediately abandoned his secular priesthood and entered a strict religious order, where he fervently prayed for the deceased until his death.

About a Soldier Whose Life was Saved by Souls in Purgatory

There was a devout soldier who had a habit of reciting prayers for the souls of the departed whenever he passed by a cemetery. One day, a hostile enemy unit spotted him and decided to kill him. Realizing the imminent danger of death, the soldier started to flee. As his escape route led him through the cemetery, he found himself amidst the graves and pondered:

"What should I do? Should I save my own life or uphold the custom of praying for the deceased?"

He didn't have much time to contemplate, as there was no time for that. He chose to recite the prayer for the souls. So, crossing himself devoutly, he began reciting the "eternal rest" prayer. Suddenly, his persecutors froze in their tracks as if petrified. They saw the soldier surrounded by an innumerable host of armed beings who clearly intended to protect him. Witnessing this overwhelming advantage, the persecutors quickly fled.

If the reader has not yet deduced it, I will explain that the multitude of armed beings surrounding our soldier were the souls who, with special permission from God, hurried to his aid, shielding him from certain death.

The Souls of the Deceased Responded 'Amen' to the Praying Priest

During the flourishing times of the Cluniac monastery, there was a monk who served as a priest and fulfilled his duties with dignity. Among his many virtues, one was that whenever he passed through a cemetery, he prayed for those resting in the graves, never forgetting that it pleases God when we remember and support the departed by offering them our merits.

One day, as he once again had to traverse the cemetery path, silently praying, he added aloud, "Requiescant in pace" - May they rest in peace. To his great astonishment, he then heard the voices of a multitude of people responding to him, saying, "Amen! Amen!"

The monk understood that these were the voices - full of gratitude - of those he had prayed for, affirming him in the belief that his actions held great value for them. From that moment on, he prayed even more fervently for the deceased, aiding and bringing relief to those who suffered, accumulating their gratitude while also acquiring merits in the eyes of God, for as Holy Scripture says, "It is a holy and wholesome thought to pray for the dead."

There is no doubt that when this monk reached the end of his earthly journey, on the other side of existence, there awaited him hosts of saints whom he had helped to ascend from the dark abyss. The gratitude of the souls in Purgatory for their benefactors is immense, and they never forget those who supported them with their prayers.

As St. Odilon Freed Many Faithful
from the Clutches of Demons

A certain monk, returning by ship from the holy city of Jerusalem, found himself on a solitary rocky islet when the winds drove the vessel to its shores. There he encountered a devout man who asked if he knew a certain Odilon, the abbot of Cluny. Once he confirmed this acquaintance, he heard these words from the hermit's mouth:

"There is a place near my dwelling where the souls in Purgatory are fiercely tormented by demons. But thanks to the prayers of the Cluniac monks and their abbot, many souls are snatched from the clutches of the devil and led into heavenly glory, which greatly angers the forces of evil. Therefore, when you return to your lands, after leaving this islet, make every effort to inform Odilon promptly, asking him to pray even more fervently and to give alms (alongside his fellow monks) for the sake of the departed, as this will greatly assist many of them."

When the pilgrim returned to his country and stood in Cluny, he recounted everything to Odilon. The abbot, in turn, decided that in all his monasteries, the 2nd of November

should be observed as "All Souls' Day," with special prayers offered for the deceased. This custom has endured until our
present times.

About How Tears Shed for the Deceased Harm Them

T here was a woman who had a son. He was very wise, very
beautiful, and distinguished by great nobility. She loved
him immensely, seeing him as the support in her old age.

However, things don't always go as we wish. It happened on
a certain day that the son passed away.

The woman's grief over the loss of her only child exceeded
all bounds, and in her unrelieved sorrow, she wept for many
days and whole weeks.

But on one occasion, it is unknown whether she experienced it in a waking state or in a half-sleep, she saw before her
a wide and comfortable path stretching through fields, mead-
ows, and groves. Beautiful flowers and lush grass grew abun-
dantly on its edges.

In the middle of that path, two youths of heavenly beauty
walked in radiant garments, while behind them, much, much
farther away, her son trudged slowly, one step at a time.

"Son!" she exclaimed upon seeing him. "Why don't you join
those youths who are far ahead of you? Surely, they are head-
ing to heavenly paradise?!"

"Yes, mother, but no matter how much I desire, I cannot accelerate. Look, here is my garment, completely soaked with your tears shed in vain after my death. It hinders my movements and becomes a great burden. Oh, mother, if instead of despairing and shedding tears, you had prayed for me, not only would I have caught up with those youths, but I would have surpassed them!"

Having said these words, he vanished into thin air, and the vision disappeared.

When the woman woke up, having reflected on the entire matter and drawn a suitable lesson from it, she never wept again for her only child.

About the Dishonest Nephew

It happened during the time when Charlemagne ruled. In his retinue, there was a certain noble, righteous, and exceedingly devout knight. When death stared him in the eyes, realizing that he could not escape paying the debt of divine justice in the purgatorial darkness, he called his nephew to his bedside, whom he held dear, and spoke these words to him:

"Listen, my dear. Since all my possessions, which I possess of noble and noble-blooded origin, include a war horse, when I pass away, sell it at the highest price you can, and distribute the money obtained in this way to the poor, with the intention of alleviating my purgatorial torments."

Having said this, he closed his eyes, never to open them again.

Although he trusted his nephew, he severely miscalculated, as instead of fulfilling the dying man's will, the nephew appropriated the war horse for himself and even boasted about possessing it.

And so, a whole year passed. Until one day, when the nephew was resting in his chamber in the evening, a figure of his deceased uncle surrounded by unearthly radiance appeared before him.

"You did not do what I had asked of you," the apparition spoke, "to save me. Because of that, I had to endure severe torments in the fire. But the voice of my complaint reached the ears of the Lord, and He, guided by mercy and justice, pardoned the remaining punishment for me, while also deciding that you will fulfill it in my place. As you can see, I am going to heaven. As for you, prepare yourself for severe suffering, which will henceforth be your constant fate."

Having said this, the apparition disappeared, and the dishonest nephew immediately fell into a severe and painful illness that plagued him until his death.

About the Punishment Suffered by a Certain Priest Who Appropriated Another's Cloak

In a certain village, a poor pilgrim, when he was dying, entrusted his entire possession, a woolen cloak, to the local priest, so that the priest would commend his soul to God in prayers.

The priest accepted the cloak, but whether due to absent-mindedness or some other reason, he quickly forgot about it and did not pray for the deceased.

Years later, the priest, driven by a special calling, entered a monastery, where he led a devout life, praying, fasting, and mortifying himself.

He did not remember that cloak we mentioned earlier, nor the pilgrim who had pleaded to God for it.

But heaven did not forget, and it happened once, by God's special permission, that our priest, while sleeping in his cell, saw himself in hell, where great tumult and commotion reigned, and demons tormented the damned in various ways.

Terrified by what he saw, he stood quietly on the side, contemplating how he could escape unnoticed from that place of torment and eternal despair.

Unfortunately, the devils spotted him, and one of them pointed at him with his finger and said:

"Look! Here is the usurper of another's cloak, deserving of payment for his sin!"

Then the demon, somehow producing that cloak, soaked it in a foul and boiling lye and struck the dishonest priest twice in the face with all his might.

At that moment, the priest woke up from his sleep, feeling an unbearable and indescribable pain, and he began to scream with all his might:

"Save me! Save me! For I am burning and dying!"

Dismayed and astonished, the monks gathered and stood by the bed of the screaming man. His entire face was burned in places down to the bone, the skin blackened and cracked, re- vealing bloody patches of flesh.

As One Holy Mass Offered Fifteen Years
of Torment Released the Deceased

Father Iwo, a Dominican, once a provincial in the Holy Land, while saying the morning prayers in the church, suddenly saw a certain monk before him dressed in filthy attire.

"Who are you and what are you seeking here?" asked Iwo.

"What? Don't you recognize me? I am indeed your friend who recently departed from life. After death, I ended up in purgatory, where I was sentenced to fifteen years of severe torment."

"Is that so?" exclaimed the provincial. He knew the deceased well and knew that during his lifetime, he was regarded as an exemplar of all the virtues of the religious order.

"Ah! The justice of God knows what it does. Truly, I deserved that solemn sentence. However, if you would be willing to show me help, which the mercy of the Most High has allowed, then pray for me in my intention."

Therefore, as soon as dawn broke, Iwo, dressed in priestly robes, proceeded to celebrate the Holy Liturgy. After consecrating the host, he spoke as follows:

"Lord! You are not more cruel than Satan. I beseech and im-plore You, by the boundless mercy of Yours, release my beloved brother from the prison of purgatory and admit him to eternal glory."

With great tears, he repeated these words multiple times, so much so that the celebration of the Holy Mass significantly lengthened.

On the following night, when Iwo was praying again in the church, he once again saw that deceased brother. This time, he was no longer in filthy garments but in shining white attire.

"It is good that by God's grace, you have obtained from the Lord a shortening of my torments, that you did not disappoint me and did not disregard my pleas. Behold, the good God has granted me further expiation of His justice and has entrusted me to you. Having been freed from purgatory, I am going in the company of blessed spirits to the heavenly homeland." Having said this, he immediately disappeared.

On the Strange Command of St. Pachomius

When St. Pachomius once visited one of the monasteries under his authority, he happened to come across the funeral of a certain monk who had led a non-virtuous life. The funeral was grand, with the singing of psalms and the burning of incense. The deceased himself was dressed in priestly robes, according to custom. When the monks saw St. Pachomius approaching, they begged him to honor the deceased by joining in the elaborate funeral. However, the pious elder commanded them as follows:

"Immediately cease the burning of incense, and remove the body from the priestly garments. Then, quietly and without fuss, lay him to rest in the ground and cover him with a burial mound."

As everyone began to express their outrage at the saint for such a seemingly unmerciful decision that, in their opinion, harmed the deceased and showed disrespect to the family, Pachomius spoke thus:

"You all know that the deceased led an unseemly life and that the Lord commands him to atone for it in purgatory (and I speak this under the inspiration of the Holy Spirit). The lavish funeral you intended to arrange would be of no help to the corpse, and it would only add additional, and by no means light, torments to the departed soul. Therefore, out of compassion for him, spare him this additional pain. Pray for him instead."

At that moment, those present at the burial understood that St. Pachomius, in making such a decision, was guided not by prejudice or disdain, but by mercy towards the deceased. Therefore, they did as he commanded, and in silence, after burying the body, each went their own way.

Speaking Ill of the Dead is Inappropriate

A certain nobleman, lying in bed and unable to sleep because it happened to be a full moon, began to ponder over the wicked life of a particular acquaintance who had recently passed away. He listed various sins and faults, refusing to see any goodness in him, and accused him only of wrongdoing. Suddenly, out of nowhere, the deceased whom our nobleman had thought so poorly of appeared before him, clearly visible in the moonlight streaming through the wide-open window.

The apparition remained silent for a while before finally speaking these words: "Friend, stop thinking ill of me, and if I have done anything wrong to you or have failed in any way, please forgive me wholeheartedly. After death, I ended up in purgatory, where I am suffering greatly. Do not cause me further pain, but rather help me through prayer."

Since the nobleman lying in bed was not easily frightened, he asked the apparition about the gravest sins for which it was enduring torment. In response, he heard: "For engaging in a duel and shedding blood in a cemetery, and for tearing the clothes off a wounded person and appropriating them for myself. And now, in the depths of purgatory, these clothes weigh heavier on me than a colossal mountain!"

When the nobleman solemnly promised to seek the aid of a respectable and virtuous hermit to pray for the deceased, the apparition revealed at the end: "In gratitude for the promised assistance, I will disclose to you what is more important to you than anything else in the world. In two years' time, counting from this moment, you will die. Prepare yourself for death. Repent so that you may avoid the fate that befell me."

After these words, the specter vanished. The prophecy came true down to the last detail, and the nobleman, taking the apparition's words to heart, transformed his former life. Having accumulated many merits, when the two years had passed, he peacefully fell asleep in the Lord.

Speaking Ill of the Dead is Unjust

A certain nobleman, lying in bed, unable to sleep because it was the night of the full moon, began to reflect on the wicked life of a certain acquaintance of his who had recently passed away. He kept inventing various sins and faults for him, not wanting to see anything good in him, and accused him of nothing but evil.

Suddenly, out of nowhere, the deceased, about whom our nobleman was thinking so badly, appeared before him, clearly visible in the moonlight that was streaming through the wide-open window. The apparition remained silent for a while, then spoke these words:

"Friend, stop thinking ill of me, and if I have done you any wrong or transgressed in any way, I sincerely ask for your forgiveness. After death, I ended up in purgatory, where I am being severely tormented. Do not add more pain to me, but rather aid me with your prayers."

Since the nobleman lying in bed was not easily frightened, he asked the apparition what sins had caused it to suffer such severe torments. In response, he heard:

"For having shed blood in a duel on a certain cemetery and for tearing off the clothes from a wounded man and appropriating them for myself. Now, these clothes weigh on me in the abyss of purgatory like a colossal mountain!"

When the nobleman solemnly promised to ask a respected and devout hermit to pray for the soul of the deceased, the apparition informed him in conclusion:

"In gratitude for the promised relief, I will reveal to you something more important to you than anything else in the world. Two years from now, counting from this moment, you will die. You have time, prepare for death. Repent so that you may avoid the fate that befell me."

Having said these words, the specter vanished.

The prophecy, in turn, was fulfilled to the letter, and the nobleman, taking the words of the apparition to heart, transformed his previous life and, accumulating many merits, peacefully passed away in the Lord when those two years had elapsed.

How the Souls of the Deceased
Assisted Prince Eusebius

T wo princes were constantly engaged in battles with each other. One hailed from Sardinia, and his name was Eusebius, while the other came from Sicily and was called Ostergis. Eusebius had a great concern for the souls in purgatory, and he supported them with numerous offerings. Moreover, he had given one of his cities to the deceased as their possession. All the income it generated was allocated for masses and alms to rescue the souls suffering in the fires of purgatory.

One day, his enemy, the Sicilian prince Ostergis, attacked that city, deceitfully seized it, and claimed it for himself. As one can imagine, Prince Eusebius, along with his faithful knights, had no intention of leaving the city in the hands of the invader. However, he feared a shameful defeat, as the enemy forces outnumbered his own.

While he was troubled by this, standing at the top of the castle tower, he suddenly noticed an immeasurable number of armed soldiers approaching his abode. An army so vast that it extended to the horizon. Each of those soldiers was clad in white armor, wearing a white cloak, holding a white banner, and riding a white horse with a white caparison.

Quickly, Eusebius sent his men to that army to inquire about their identity and purpose. When the messengers returned, they delivered the most pleasant news the prince could hope for:

"Your Highness, God sends His hosts to help you reclaim the city, which you offered for the benefit of the souls suffering in purgatory."

And so it happened. Frightened by the countless number of armed soldiers who sternly demanded that they quickly abandon the seized city and territory, the invader obediently withdrew to his own country.

Meanwhile, Eusebius, driven by curiosity, dared to ask the soldiers who they were, wondering if they were not angels themselves. But they denied:

"We are the souls of the deceased who, thanks to your kindness and alms, have attained eternal glory."

Then, bidding farewell to the prince, the departed souls departed the way they had come.

Nepotism, the Cause of Purgatorial Torment

There was an abbot who was highly respected among his subordinate monks. He stood out due to his genuine and not pretended piety, leading an extraordinarily virtuous life. As he approached his death, he decided, out of family considerations, to persuade the monks to choose his relative as the new abbot when the time came.

After the old abbot passed away, his wish was fulfilled, and the relative was appointed as the new abbot. Since the deceased abbot had lived a saintly life and died with sanctity, everyone believed that he had gone straight to heavenly bliss. However, on a certain occasion, he appeared to his relative, lamenting terribly.

Shocked with fear, the relative asked for the reason behind the complaints. The deceased abbot replied:

"I moan and lament because I am burning!"

"You are burning? Why?"

"It is because, influenced by affection toward you, instead of heeding God's voice, I blinded myself and recommended you as my successor. Due to this very reason, God condemned me to purgatory."

Sincere Remorse for Sins Saves Even
a Criminal from Hell

A young man of noble descent, driven more by fancy than calling, decided to join the Cistercian order and, after taking his vows, was ordained as a priest. His relative, who was the bishop of the local diocese, unsuccessfully tried to dissuade him from this plan. Nothing helped.

A year passed, and our young monk grew tired of monastic life. He abandoned the monastery, took off his habit, and donned secular attire. However, he felt ashamed to return to his parents, knowing that he had not persevered in the order. Unsure of what to do, he joined a band of robbers and quickly became skilled in their criminal trade, becoming the most ruthless among the criminals, even terrifying the most cruel among them.

As everyone's life has its end, the wicked monk's life also came to a close. In a certain skirmish, mortally wounded, he began to bid farewell to earthly existence. But before his death, his conscience started tormenting him, and he felt genuine and sincere remorse for his sins. He asked his comrades to bring a priest to him so that he could confess his sins and, having obtained absolution, pass on to the other side of life.

When the parish priest arrived, our monk made a sincere confession before him. He declared that he was a priest who had run away from the Cistercian monastery. He admitted that during all those years as a member of the band of robbers, he had stained his hands with the blood of hundreds of innocent people, taking their lives and plundering their belongings. He also confessed to having raped many virgins and married women, not sparing even nuns. Now, facing death, he sincerely regretted the evil he had committed and begged for absolution with tears in his eyes.

The priest, who listened to this confession, had a strangely hardened heart because, instead of granting absolution, he said to the penitent:

"Your sins are so terrible that they are not worthy of forgiveness."

The dying man, in vain, repented and pleaded for mercy and absolution. The priest remained stubborn and refused to even consider granting absolution.

Then the former monk said:

"If that's the case, at least give me the Body of the Lord as sustenance for the eternal journey."

"Have you gone mad?!" exclaimed the priest. "If I refuse to absolve you, why would I administer Holy Communion to you?!"

"Well, if that's the case, at least allow me to impose a penance upon myself for my countless and horrendous crimes," replied the monk-robber, and with these words on his lips, he passed away.

When the bishop cousin heard of his death, moved by compassion, he ordered that prayers be said for the deceased in all the churches and monasteries under his jurisdiction for a year, and this order was diligently fulfilled.

When that year came to an end, after the Mass celebrated by the bishop, the deceased appeared to him while standing behind the altar. He was pale, emaciated, miserable, dressed in mourning attire.

When the bishop asked how he was doing and where he came from, he replied:

"I am tormented and come from suffering, but I thank you for your love because, due to your alms and prayers during this year, and for the benefit of the Holy Church, my thousand years of torment in purgatory have been shortened. And if you continue to have care for me for another year, I will be completely freed from punishment."

Upon hearing this, the bishop rejoiced and thanked God, and naturally, he ordered another year of prayers for the deceased monk-robber.

And when that year had passed, and the bishop celebrated Holy Mass, the departed appeared to him once again and said:

"Thanks to your persistence and mercy, I have been saved from the torments of purgatory and am now entering the wedding feast of my Lord. And those two years of your prayers and offerings are counted for me as two thousand years."

Since then, the bishop never saw him again.

Years of Suffering in the Body are Nothing Compared to a Single Moment in Purgatory

O nce upon a time, a certain man fell ill and experienced excruciating pain. His suffering was so severe that every day he earnestly begged God to send him death so that he would no longer have to endure it.

Instead of death, God sent an angel to him, who said the following:

"Our Almighty Creator gives you a choice: either death and three days in purgatory afterward, or another year of life in your body, enduring the same suffering you are experiencing now. However, once that year is over, you will go straight to heaven."

A year or three days? The sick man didn't hesitate for long. He chose purgatory.

So his wish was granted. He died and found himself in the fiery abyss. After one day had passed, the angel visited him again and asked if he still stood by his previous decision.

But our deceased, with indignation, exclaimed that he had been deceived because he had already been roasting in the fire for not just one day, as the angel claimed, but for countless ages.

Unperturbed by these reproaches, the messenger of the Lord explained to the soul as follows:

"It is not the length of time that deceives you but the unbearable agony of the torment. In reality, you have only spent a single day in this place of torment! Do not fear, for the Lord has shown mercy upon you and allowed you to return to your body."

How eagerly our departed one agreed to this! And just as promised, he suffered due to his illness for the entire year, and then he was taken straight to paradise.

Purgatory as a River of Boiling Tar

Describing a strange vision in a letter to the sister of a resurrected man, Yinfridus or Bonifacius says the following:

Your deceased brother saw a place of wondrous delight where beautiful people were enjoying themselves and celebrating. And from this place, a peculiar sweet fragrance reached his nostrils.

The accompanying angel claimed that this was a part of heaven.

But besides heaven, he also saw a river flowing with streams of boiling tar, and instead of a bridge, there was only a trunk of a dry tree laid across its banks.

Souls would pass over this trunk, and many of them would fall from it. Some would immerse themselves completely in the boiling tar, others up to their waist, some up to their knees, and still others only up to their ankles. Afterward, they would emerge purified and radiant on the other side.

The guiding angel explained that these were the souls un-dergoing the purifying torments of purgatory so that they could later, in a worthy manner, attain eternal glory and dwell in the holy city, the heavenly Jerusalem.

On the Soul that Rejoiced at the Birth of a Child

A certain man, who was once dead but came back to life, later recounted an event that he witnessed while in purgatory. He described it as follows:

There was a soul, engulfed in the greatest fire, that suddenly exclaimed, "Oh, what happiness has befallen me!"

When asked about the reason for this joy, the soul replied, "The angels have revealed to me that at this very moment, a child has been born who will become a priest, and during his first Mass, he will deliver me from the torments of purgatory."

A Man Devoted to Hunting Suffers Great Torment

A devout man, overcome with enthusiasm, saw a soldier immersed in purgatory. Although this soldier was pure, virtuous, diligent, and lived a pious life, he ended up in the fire because he excessively loved hunting.

His punishment appeared as follows:

A bird sat on his hand, pecking at his face, arm, and hands, tearing strips of flesh from those areas and tormenting him cruelly as a form of penance.

When the man, filled with astonishment, asked why he was suffering, considering his righteous life and adherence to God's commandments, the soldier replied:

"I have observed God's commandments, never deceiving anyone in even the slightest matter. However, I have loved hunting with birds above all else, almost making it a deity. It is for this reason that I endure such a cruel and heavy torment. It will continue until I am completely purified."

The penitent fell silent for a moment, and then he began to speak again:

"If you have compassion for me, please beseech the Lord on my behalf and also tell my children and relatives to save me

through alms, prayers, and holy offerings, for I suffer indescribable torments."

The man we mentioned at the beginning, upon coming out
of his state of enthusiasm, did not forget the plea of the repen-
tant soul. He fulfilled it to the letter, gaining gratitude from
the soul and merit in the eyes of God.

The Vision of St. Bridget

I "saw a dark and terrifying place, and above it, a soul as if clothed in a body... Frightful flames rose from the depths towards her and burned her with such force that the pores of her body seemed to be open veins from which fire spouted... And I heard the soul crying out five times: Woe!... Woe to me, for I loved the Lord God so little, even though I was generously bestowed with His graces!... Woe to me, for I did not fear His justice! Woe to me, for I sought disgraceful pleasures of the flesh! Woe to me, for I desired wealth, honors, and glory! Woe to me, for I listened to you, Satan, who led me astray".

At that moment, an angel said to me: This abyss is hell; whoever enters it will never behold God. Above this abyss lies the place of the greatest purgatorial torments. The soul you see suffers the burning of consuming fire... it is saddened by darkness... greatly humiliated and ashamed, and terrified by the sight of demons. Yet, in all these torments, it is consoled by the remembrance of its good deeds. There is a second place of purification where the torments are less severe. The souls remaining there are like the weak, slowly regaining strength and beauty. Finally, there is a third place, higher than the others, a spiritual purgatory, where the souls suffer only the terrible torment of longing for God. (*O czyśćcu i duszach czyśćcowych*, [w:] „Głosy Katolickie", 1901, pp. 8-9).

The Revelation in Zamora

In a Dominican monastery in Spain, a friar of St. Francis, a friend of one of the Dominican Fathers, appeared in blazing fire, telling him that he was saved by God's mercy but suffered greatly in purgatory for numerous minor faults for which he did not repent during his lifetime. He added, 'Nothing in the world can give you an idea of this terrible torment!' Then he placed his hand on the table, and immediately a deep mark was burned as if by hot iron. This table was preserved as a memento and is still shown to this day. (*O czyśćcu i duszach czyśćcowych*, p. 9).

The Vision of Father Hipolito Scealvo

In the life of the pious Father Hipolito Scealvo, a Capuchin monk, it is recorded that he had a great devotion to the souls in purgatory. Among other practices, every morning at dawn, he recited the Office for the deceased. One day, while he was praying in the choir for the soul of a novice who had passed away the previous night, that deceased novice appeared to him in vivid fiery flames. The soul told him that by God's command, he had come to confess his guilt and ask for penance, which Father Scealvo, as his superior, was to assign to him.

Father Scealvo immediately assigned him penance until prime, which is the first prayer recited by the monks in the morning choir. In response, the soul in purgatory exclaimed, "Oh heart without mercy, oh father without compassion for your suffering son. Can such a small punishment be given for a minor fault? Don't you know how dreadful the torments of purgatorial fire are? Oh penance without mercy!"

Father Scealvo was deeply shaken! He came up with an idea and immediately ran to the bell and called the monks to the church. He shared his vision with them and instructed them to recite the prime immediately. For the 20 years he lived after that event, he could not forget it and often narrated it in his sermons. (*O czyśccu i duszach czyśccowych*, p. 9-10).

The Apparition of Anna Potocka

In the Benedictine Nuns' convent in Przemyśl, the soul of Anna Potocka, the wife of Salezy Potocki from Krystynopol, appeared several times to one of the nuns. The last time, in the presence of the Episcopal commission, as evidence of the truth, she burned a cross onto the nun's hand with fire. A detailed description of this, along with the records of the Episcopal commission, was read in the chronicles of the Basilian Fathers in Krystynopol, where Potocka's body rests. (*O czyśćcu i duszach czyśćcowych*, p. 10-11).

The Penitent Benedictine

In the abbey of the Benedictine Fathers in Latrobe, America, from September 18th, 1859, a deceased Benedictine appeared for 2 months and said in the presence of another brother that he had been suffering in Purgatory for 77 years for not celebrating seven obligatory Masses, and he requested that they be celebrated. X. Abbot Wimmer announced this in the newspapers. (*O czyśćcu i duszach czyśćcowych*, p. 11).

The Apparition of Countess Łosiowa

In Brzuchowice near Przemyślany, on July 19, 1750, the soul of Helena Łosiowa, née Cetner, who had passed away on May 26 of the same year, appeared in broad daylight, seeking help and, as proof of the truth, burned a mark of her hand on the table. Her son, Count Józef Łoś, donated this table with a detailed description on a marble plaque to the parish church in Przemyślany, where it remains to this day. (*O czyśćcu i duszach czyśćcowych*, p. 10)

The Apparition of Teresa Giotti

In the year 1859, at the convent of the Franciscan Sisters in Foligno, near Assisi, the soul of the deceased nun Teresa Giotti appeared to her successor in office, Sister Anna Felicja. She appeared engulfed in flames and, as proof of the truth, burned the mark of her hand on the doors. She spoke of the terrible torments she endures and that she is condemned to 40 years in purgatory for minor transgressions against the poverty of the convent and for not loving her fellow sisters with an equal heart. She stated that she comes by the command of God's mercy to seek help and rescue. After several days, during which many prayers and acts of penance, especially Masses, were offered for her, she appeared again, expressing gratitude for the assistance and declaring that she has been delivered from purgatory and is going to heaven. At the request of the Bishop of Foligno and the city authorities, her grave was opened, her body was removed, and the hand of the deceased was placed against the burned mark on the doors. It was reported that the burned mark perfectly matched the delicate hand of the deceased nun. The doors with the burned mark are preserved to this day in the church. Bishop Segur personally witnessed these doors and the burned mark on them, and he extensively described the event in his work: 'There is a Hell.'" (*O czyśćcu i duszach czyśćcowych*, pp. 11-12)

The Apparition of Antoni Korso

Brother Korso, a holy member of the Franciscan order, who was widely known as an earthly angel due to his saintly life, did not go straight to heaven after death. With God's permission, he appeared very sad to the infirmarian of the monastery. After recovering from fear, the infirmarian exclaimed, "What is this? Brother Antoni in purgatory? I thought you were already in the heavenly glory... What do you suffer?"

"Oh," replied Brother Antoni, "I endure a terrible torment of longing for God, for I am not yet admitted to behold Him. And even if I were to endure all the physical torments of hell, they would be more bearable to me than the fire that burns and torments me... It is a severe hunger, a consuming desire, by which the soul withers and wastes away, unable to die. No mortal can comprehend this dreadful agony. Pray for me and commend me to the prayers of all the brothers. Help me to unite with God! Give me God!... Ah! give me my God!" (*O czyśćcu i duszach czyśćcowych*, pp. 24-25)

The Penitent Frenchwoman

In a certain convent in France, in the year 1863, one of the nuns, as she was leaving her cell, saw a great light and heard someone calling her by name. Initially, she was very frightened and did not respond. But then, seeing a human figure before her, she gathered courage and asked the apparition who they were and what they needed. "I am your sister, Zofia... Do you remember how you were told yesterday that you resemble Sister Zofia, who passed away 7 years ago? And in your spirit, you asked for the cause of my situation, whether I am in heaven or if I am detained in purgatory. You offered indulgences for me the next day. Due to this act of love, the Lord allows me to ask for your support, which I am in great need of. Ah! Pray for me and ask the superiors to recommend me to the prayers of the congregation so that I may behold God as soon as possible.

After a few days, the nun heard the call again and saw the light surrounding her, and the soul once again pleaded for help to be released from her longing, adding that although everything prescribed by the monastic rule for deceased sisters had been performed on her behalf, no one remembered her anymore. "If you show me mercy, I will be grateful to you for all eternity." Various prayers were then offered and many Masses and Holy Communions were dedicated for her. From that time on, the nun continuously saw the presence of Sister Zofia as if in a mist. The more they prayed, the clearer and brighter the apparition became. Three other nuns also witnessed this soul before her final deliverance. Finally, after several weeks, she appeared for the last time, shining with the glory of heaven, as she was about to enter paradise. (*O czyśćcu i duszach czyśćcowych*, pp. 25-26)

The Vision of St. Gertrude

After death, the soul of a very (...) virtuous nun appeared to St. Gertrude, saying that she is detained in purgatory because during her final illness, she sought excessive relief and comforts. (*O czyśćcu i duszach czyśćcowych*, p. 30).

The Revelation of Blessed Veronica

In the accounts of the Bollandists, we read about the life of Blessed Veronica, who had terrifying visions of the purgatorial sufferings of religious souls due to minor disobediences, negligence in spiritual exercises, and idle chatter, among other things. After this vision, she was overcome with sadness, immense pain, and terror, and began to cry out in a mournful voice, 'Ah, ah! What terrible torments I have witnessed today, what dreadful tortures!' As she spoke, she fell into a high fever, and as a sign of truth, marks the size of a hand, resembling fiery flames, appeared all over her body. (*O czyśćcu i duszach czyśćcowych*, p. 30-31).

The Apparition of Brother Constantine

Brother Constantine, a member of the Capuchin Order, a man known for his holiness of life and miracles both during his lifetime and after his death, appeared a few days after his demise to one of the priests of the same order. When asked about the afterlife, he replied, 'Ah, brother, how terrifying are the judgments of the Lord! They are entirely different from human judgments and opinions! What seemed to the living as virtue is often judged as sin by the Lord God, who measures everything justly! Although I obtained salvation through the mercy of God, I spent three days in purgatory, which, I truthfully tell you, felt like three thousand years, all for certain mistakes that I considered mere faults during my earthly life. (*O czyśćcu i duszach czyśćcowych*, p. 32-33).

The Extraordinary Experience of Prince Lubomirski

Prince Lubomirski, as he himself recounted, had written a book against the immortality of the soul and was about to submit it for printing... when he came across a peasant woman in his garden, crying bitterly. She threw herself at his feet and tearfully begged him for alms to pay for her husband's funeral and for a Holy Mass for the soul of her recently deceased spouse, mentioning that he might need help in purgatory, while she, being poor, couldn't afford even a single Mass. Though the prince did not believe in the immortality of the soul, he was somehow moved and reluctantly gave her a gold coin.

Five days later, while the prince was reading his godless manuscript in his room, he saw the peasant standing before him. The man said, 'I have come to thank you for your charity, Prince. I am the husband of that poor woman who asked you for alms a few days ago, to have a Holy Mass said for my soul... You showed her and me mercy, and by God's permission, I am allowed to come and thank you.' With those words, he disappeared. The prince was deeply terrified and moved. He repented, burned his manuscript, and from then on became a model of Christian virtues and acts of mercy. (*O czyśćcu i duszach czyśćcowych*, p. 43).

Contents

Introduction 5

Death Is Not The End Of Existence 8

Detailed Judgment – It Will Reveal The Deeds
Of The Soul, Weigh And Pass Judgment 14

And When You Die, You Will Receive Your Payment 17

Purgatory 19

Can The Deceased Manifest Themselves
To The Living? 25

Purgatory Tales 28

Caring for the soul 29

Memory of Souls about Us 31

Miracles of God's mercy through the intercession
of the souls in purgatory 33

Almsgiving for the deceased will not go unrewarded 35

About soldiers asking for assistance after death 38

About the monk who ended up in purgatory
due to negligence in praying for the deceased 40

The value of the Holy Sacrifice
for the souls in purgatory 42

On the torments suffered
by unworthy monks in purgatory 43

An hour in purgatory feels like an eternity 44

The Hour in Purgatory Seems Like Eternity 45

About How Heavy the Torments of Purgatory Are 47

Purgatory According to St. Frances of Rome 48

Purgatory according to St. Joanna of Jesus-Mary 49

How Blessed Sister Joanna of Jesus Mary Helped
the Souls in Purgatory 50

Purgatory in the Revelations of St. Bridget of Sweden 53

Vision of Purgatory in the Revelations of St. Bridget 56

On the Terrible Torments of a Soul,
as Seen by St. Bridget 56

Saint Sister Faustina Kowalska sees a soul
suffering in torment 58

The true story of a strange apparition
of the deceased 60

How St. Christina Penance to Relieve the Suffering
of Souls in Purgatory 63

The Heavy Torment of a Monk who,
Unworthy of It, Desired to Become a Deacon 65

The Souls of the Deceased Joyfully Welcome Those
Who Supported Them in Life 67

About a Soldier Whose Life was Saved
by Souls in Purgatory **69**

The Souls of the Deceased Responded 'Amen'
to the Praying Priest **71**

As St. Odilon Freed Many Faithful
from the Clutches of Demons **73**

About How Tears Shed
for the Deceased Harm Them **75**

About the Dishonest Nephew **77**

About the Punishment Suffered by a Certain Priest
Who Appropriated Another's Cloak **79**

As One Holy Mass Offered Fifteen Years
of Torment Released the Deceased **81**

On the Strange Command of St. Pachomius **83**

Speaking Ill of the Dead is Inappropriate **85**

Speaking Ill of the Dead is Unjust **87**

How the Souls of the Deceased
Assisted Prince Eusebius **89**

Nepotism, the Cause of Purgatorial Torment **91**

Sincere Remorse for Sins Saves Even
a Criminal from Hell **92**

Years of Suffering in the Body are Nothing
Compared to a Single Moment in Purgatory **95**

Purgatory as a River of Boiling Tar **97**

On the Soul that Rejoiced at the Birth of a Child **99**

A Man Devoted to Hunting Suffers Great Torment **100**

The Vision of St. Bridget 102

The Revelation in Zamora 104

The Vision of Father Hipolito Scealvo 105

The Apparition of Anna Potocka 107

The Penitent Benedictine 108

The Apparition of Countess Łosiowa 109

The Apparition of Teresa Giotti 110

The Apparition of Antoni Korso 112

The Penitent Frenchwoman 113

The Vision of St. Gertrude 115

The Revelation of Blessed Veronica 116

The Apparition of Brother Constantine 117

The Extraordinary Experience
of Prince Lubomirski 118